Command Line for MacOS Terminal

*An Introduction to Understanding and Using
Command Line For MacOS Terminal*

James Little

Table of Contents

Introduction

Thank you for taking the time to download this book: Command Line For MacOS Terminal.

This book covers the topic of the command line for MacOS and how you can learn how to use it. At the completion of this book, you will have a good understanding of the terminal and the command line for your Mac computer, and you will be able to complete some of your own commands through this system in no time.

While most people are used to working with the graphical user interface (the kind where they just click on the icons to tell the computer how to behave, working with the terminal can be so much better. This is going to help you to command the computer how to behave much easier, can help you complete more complex tasks, and can even make it easier to troubleshoot what is going on with your computer.

Working with the terminal and the command line can take some time to get used to, but it is one of the best options out there. And this guidebook will help you to get it all set up and ready to go. After practicing some of the different commands that you can use, you will find that it is actually easier to work with the command line than it is to work without it. This guidebook will provide you with all the tools and the practice commands that you need to get the hang of it and start using it for your own needs.

When you are ready to start understanding your computer in a way that you never imagined before, and you want to be able to see the inner workings of it while still being in control, make sure to check out this guidebook to learn how to get started with the command line on the Mac operating system.

Once again, thanks for downloading this book, I hope you find it to be helpful!

Chapter 1
The Basics of the MacOS Command Line

Working with the command line can be a bit scary when you are first getting started. It does look different than what you may be used to with the Linux system and with the Windows operating system. You may be starting out with the MacOS and have no idea how to work with the command line to start with. It doesn't help when you open up the instructions that tell you how to get started, and you see a long list of phrases and words that make no sense.

The good news is that the MacOS command line is really not as difficult to use as it may appear in the beginning. Whether you are a beginner or you have been working with programming for a long time, you will be able to work with the MacOS command line and get things done in no time. Let's get started with some of the basics that come with the MacOS command line to help you to get started.

Opening up the command line

The first thing that we need to learn how to do is open up the command line. You will need to find the command line so that you can use it in the ways that you would like. This is a simple process. You will just need to open up the terminal. Go ahead and turn on your Mac computer. When it is ready, you can open up the Applications folder followed by the Utilities folder. Inside the Utilities folder, you should see the Terminal application.

At this point, you may want to consider adding the Terminal application to your dock so that it is easier to find and you will not have to spend so much time searching for it. Another way that you can do this to save time is to launch your terminal by doing the Spotlight search and then looking for "terminal". Any of these methods will open up the terminal for you so that you can start working.

The parts of the console

Before you can get a lot of work done on your console, there are a few parts that need to come together. Some of the terms that you should know to help all of this make sense include:

- Console: The console is the system as a whole. The console is going to include the command line, as well as any output that shows up from the previous commands.

- Command line: When you are looking at the command line, you are looking at the actual line inside of the console where you will type in the commands.

- Prompt: The prompt is going to be the beginning of your command line. It is often going to hold onto some contextual information. This may include information like where you are and who you are. This prompt is going to end with a $. Once the prompt is done, you will start typing in your commands.

- Terminal: The terminal is going to be the interface of the console. It is the program that you will use to interact with the console. When you are working with what is known as the terminal emulator, you will get the experience of typing inside an old terminal while still working in the modern graphical operating system.

Running a command

When you are on the console, you will want to learn how to run a command. Most of the commands that you will do on the MacOS will have three main parts. These three parts include the program, the options, and the arguments.

The program is going to be like the verb of your command. The program will be in charge of telling the program what you want it to do. There are a lot of different programs that you can use based on what you would like your console to do.

Next are the options and you can think about them like the adverb of your command. They are the modifiers of the program and can make changes in how it runs. These options are completely optional, so you can run a program without one of them. Each command will have its own options though so you will have to be careful about adding these in. Most often the order of your options is not going to matter that much, but there are times when they will, and we can discuss those later.

And finally, the arguments are whatever is left. They are considered the objects of the sentence, and they will tell the command what to act on. Each program will have a different argument, and it is going to matter the order of the arguments or the command can get confused.

When you are looking to create a new program, or you are working on controlling how your computer works, you need to make sure that you can bring out the command line and make it work the way that you want. The MacOS command line is going to be a little bit different than some of the other command lines that you may have used in the past, but it can be really powerful and can help you to write out some unique codes that are easy and fun to work with.

Chapter 2
The Different Parts to Know

Getting started with programming can be a lot of fun. There are a lot of different commands that you can give to your computer, whether you are looking to open up and move files around, or you are looking to write one of your own codes. Before you get started with working with the command line, it is important to know some of the important parts that come with the command line on the MacOS.

What is a command line?

The first thing that we are going to take a look at is the command line. This is the seat of power when it comes to running your computer. When you use the command line, you can tell the computer exactly what you want it to do. Whether you want to get it to open up a file, to create a new program, or do something else, the command line is going to help you to get it done. However, while you can get a lot of power from the command line, these can actually complex and will take some time to learn how to do.

To keep things simple, the command line is just going to be the place where you will type in the commands that you want to give to the computer. As long as you write out a command that the computer can understand, it will execute that command.

One thing to note is that the computer is not going to speak English or any other language that humans know, even though there are some elements that are recognizable. This means that you will need to learn a new language, the language of the computer, before you can give these commands.

Most people do not use this command line very often. They just click on the little icons to do the work for them. They also don't have many opportunities to write a new program or any chance to tell the computer a specific command so they may not know how to find the command line.

This command line is going to be present in different locations based on the operating system that is found on your computer. When it comes to the Mac command line, you will use a program that is known as Terminal. It is found under the /Applications/Utilities.

What is a shell?

The next part that you are going to work with when programming is the shell. The shell is the user interface that allows you to access the services of an operating system. The shell is either going to be a graphical user interface or the command line interface, depending on the role of the computer.

When we are talking about the graphical user interface, this is what most people use when they are on their computers. If you are on the desktop and there are a lot of icons there for you to click on, then you are working with a graphical user interface. This is easier to use for most people and if you don't want to create your own programs or do anything more technical with your computer, then working with this interface is fine.

However, if you are looking to write out your own codes and to make sure that your computer does exactly what you want you would use with the command line interface. In this case, the shell is going to be the screen where you can write out the codes that you want to work with.

What is the terminal?

The terminal is the interface where you can type out your codes and then get the computer to execute the commands that you want to be done. When you open up the command line, you will receive a little black box that should be empty when it is first opened. You will then be able to type inside of it to tell the computer how to behave. The place where you are typing these commands will be the terminal.

How are Ubuntu and MacOS similar and different?

If you have done some programming in the past, it is likely that you have worked with Ubuntu, or Linux, in the past. This is one of the most popular command lines to use because it can work on almost any kind of computer. There are some issues with using MacOS and Windows OS for programming; often when you make a program on one of those systems, they will have trouble working on the others in some cases.

However, when you work on the Linux system, this command line can work on programs that can work on all the other major systems as well. This makes it one of the most popular systems to use to make a program that you want.

You will see that the MacOS is actually pretty similar to working with the Ubuntu system. The MacOS is similar in simplicity, and the window dialogs tend to be really similar as well. When it comes to usability, both of these operating systems are going to be pretty similar.

You will find that Mac OS is like a special kernel of Ubuntu, and most of the differences between the two come up because Apple wants to make sure that none of the programming or software is considered open source. Linux is considered an open-sourced platform, which means that anyone can use it for free, to make changes, and to improve upon the software whenever they want, without having to get some special licenses or pay extra money. With Mac OS, you will find that it is closed source, so you are not able to make these changes.

Overall, these two systems are going to be very similar, and they are very compatible. You could technically take a Linux packaging system into the MacOS, and it will work just fine.

While there are some differences that come with Ubuntu and the MacOS, they do work together very well. The main difference is that you will not be able to get the MacOS for free and you will not be able to make changes to the source code like you can with Linux. Otherwise, they are compatible with each other and if you have worked with Linux, or you would like to bring your Linux program into the MacOS terminal, this is easy to do as the two are very similar.

Chapter 3
The Basics of the MacOS Terminal

If you are looking for a way to work directly with the system on your computer, rather than having to deal with the clunky graphical user interfaces, then you will want to work with the command line. This may seem a little bit complicated when you first get started, but in reality, it can really make life simpler. You will be able to type in the exact thing that you want to get done, and you will not need to worry about searching through the computer to find what you want.

Looking at the command line is not something that most people are used to doing, but starting out with the basics will make it a little bit easier. Once you get going, you will see that the command line is not all that different from the graphical world that you may use on your computer in most cases. In addition, learning how the terminal works will help to give you a better understanding of how the Mac works behind the scenes and makes it easier for you to troubleshoot any issues that come up. Let's take a look at some of the basics of the MacOS terminal to help you get used to working with it.

What is the Mac terminal?

There are very few things that are as misunderstood as the Mac terminal. Most people will work with the graphical user interface so that they can just click on the icons on their desktop and get things done. But working with the terminal to create specific commands will make working with your Mac easier than ever before. If you have a command that would be cumbersome or would need some extra software to complete, or you would like to troubleshoot a problem on your computer, then working with the terminal can make things easier.

First, you must understand that the terminal is simply an application available on your computer. You can launch it just like you do with other applications and once you do, you will see a UNIX command line environment, which is known as a shell. There are a variety of shells that you can work with, but the one that is found on Apple computers is known as Bash.

The top of the terminal window is going to contain the title bar which will display the name of the current user (you), the shell that is being used, and the size of your window in pixels. If you take a look at the command line, you will see that each of them will start with the name of your Mac and this will be followed by your name or the name of the current user.

It is possible to have different shells in the terminal, but you will have to take the time to install those. Commands in UNIX are going to be specific to their shell, so you will want to make sure that you are using the right shell for the commands that you want, or the computer may be confused.

Using a terminal on your Mac

Once you get to using the terminal, you will find that it is pretty easy. You will get to the command line, type out your command, and then press Return to get the computer to execute that command. There are a couple of rules that you should remember when you are working with the command line interface. The first one is that all characters, even spaces, will matter. So, if you take a command from a book, website, or another source, you must make sure that it is typed the right way, or it may not work.

It is possible to rerun some of the previous commands that you have without needing to retype them. To do this, you would just need to use the up arrow to find the command and then press on Return. You can also interrupt any of the commands that you are using by pressing Control-C.

Commands

You will find that there are a variety of commands that you can use. To see which commands are available, you will just need to hold down the Escape key and then press Y when the computer asks if you would like to display a specific number of options. Then you will receive a list of commands, along with their meanings right by them. If you press on the spacebar, there will be more commands to load. When you are done looking at the commands, you can just press Q, and it takes you back to the command prompt.

Unix has placed a manual into the system, and you can call it up inside of your terminal if you need some information about a specific command. To use this manual, you would just need to type in "man [command]" The command is going to be the name of the command that you want to learn more about.

Locations

When you type in a new command in your terminal, it will automatically execute in your current location. You can change this, but you must specifically state this in your command to happen. When you start up a new terminal window, that location will be the top level of your Home directory so all commands will be relative to that location.

If you want to change up the location before doing one of your commands, you will use the command "cd" followed by the path of the location you wish to move to. If you would like to end up back at your default location, you would need to type "cd~/" If you would like to see a list of all the folders and files that are in your current location by simply typing in "ls"

Choosing your terminal emulator

Before you can start working on the command line, you need to pick out the terminal emulator that you want to work with.

There are various emulators that you can pick from based on the interfaces and features that you want. You will find that there are limited options when it comes to terminals with OS X, but if you want to keep things simple, you can work with the terminal app that comes with your computer. It doesn't have a lot of features on it, but it does offer pane splitting to view a few inputs at the same time, a few color schemes to personalize it, and some tabs.

There are some users who would like to have a bit more power when it comes to their terminal. A good one to work with is the iTerm2. It is free so you won't have to worry about having to pay a lot of extra money, and it has a lot of options. In addition to the features that you can find with the default terminal above, you will also be able to get customizable profiles, enhanced pane splitting, and more.

Working with your terminal can be an exciting way to interact with your computer. While there are many users, who like to work with the graphical interface because then they don't need to worry about learning commands, the command line, and the terminal, make it easier to control what is going on in your computer. You can take on more complex things on your computer, and even deal with troubleshooting better when you work with a command line terminal.

Chapter 4
Why Would I Want to Use the Command Line and the Terminal

It is common for most people to get on their computers and never use the command line at all. This is true whether they are using a Windows computer, a Linux computer, or a Mac computer. They see the command line as something that only computer programmers and those who really know how to work on a computer would use. They don't think that it is worth their time to know how to make this command line work and they miss out on a lot of the power that they could yield to their computers. Instead, they focus on using the graphical user interface.

This may make life easier since you just need to click on the icon rather than learning any commands along the way, but there is just so much that you can do with a command line that it is definitely worth your time to learn. Let's take a look at some of the different reasons why you would want to consider learning how to use the command line, and how to write commands in the terminal, rather than sticking with the graphical user interface that you currently use.

Adds more power

When you start using your command line, you will be surprised by how much power is behind it. This command line is going to make it easier for you to do tasks that may have seemed impossible before. While some commands may have taken a lot of searching and button clicking before, the command line will allow you to get it done with a few keystrokes.

You do not need to worry about the command line being too difficult. It does take a little bit of time to learn how the commands work, but whether you are a beginner or someone who has been working with command lines and programming in the past, you will find that it is really easy to learn. Once you learn a few commands (and we will discuss a few of these commands throughout this book), you will be able to hold all the power of the command line in your hands.

Helps you to troubleshoot your computer

One reason that a lot of people will learn how to use the command line is that it can make it easier to troubleshoot any issues that come up on the computer. Whether your computer is brand new or you have owned it for some time, there are likely problems that can come up with it that will slow down the system, make it not work properly, or something else.

Trying to troubleshoot your computer with the graphical user interface can make it really hard for you to troubleshoot what is going on in the system. You can give it a try, but it is likely that you will just end up frustrated in the long run. If you have ever taken your computer in to a professional to fix an issue, you will notice that they will bring up this command line to help them fix it for you.

Once you learn how to work with the command line, you will be able to do your own troubleshooting, even if you do not have a lot of experience working with computers. This command line will let you look behind the scenes of your computer and see things that were not possible before. You may still need the help of a professional if you have a major issue on the computer, but with some of the little ones, you may be able to do some of the work on your own.

Easier to do complex tasks and commands

You will find that it is actually easier to complete some of the tasks that you want on your computer when you can work with the command line. You may be used to working with the graphical interface and just click on the icon that you want to use. For some of the tasks that you want to complete, you will find that this is much easier. But there are a lot of tasks that should be pretty easy, but if you don't use the command line, you will find that they are really difficult.

When you are working with the command line, you can just tell the computer exactly what you would like it to do. There isn't any searching around to find what you want or any guessing about whether you are doing it the right way or not. You just have to learn a few simple commands, and it will all be taken care of for you.

Working with the command line may not be something that you are used to working with, but it is actually pretty simple. It will allow you to tell the computer exactly what you would like it to do and can just make things so much easier once you learn how to make it work.

Chapter 5
How to Navigate the Mac's File System

Navigating inside of your terminal is pretty simple. You will be able to do a few different commands, and then all the world of your computer will be at your fingertips. Whether you are trying to list out all of the folders that are on your system or you want to be able to navigate around the terminal, the commands in this chapter will help you to get it done.

Navigating the system

It is important to have an idea of how to navigate your filesystem. You will find that there are two commands that are used quite a bit. These include ls (lst) and cd (change directory). These commands are going to be used to list the contents of a directory as well as moving one directory to another.

When you open up your terminal, no matter which one you want to use, you will be placed in the home directory. This will usually be under your name. To understand how this works and relates to the GUI equivalent, you can open up a new Finder window and then select your name on the column on the left. You should then see a few different folders such as "Documents," "Desktop," and "Applications."

Looking at this same column, you can select the hard drive of the computer in "Devices." This is going to be considered the lowest level that you can get in the filesystem, and it is called the root. You will showcase this in command line terms with the "/" symbol. The root directory is going to contain all of the files that are needed to get the operating system to work, so unless you really know what you are doing, do not spend time messing around here or your computer will not work properly.

Listing the directories

Now that the terminal window is open, you can type in "ls" to list the files that are present in your home directory. You should be able to see all of the directories that are there by default on the OS X system such as "Music," "Movies," "Documents," and "Downloads". If you type in the command "Is -a", it is going to activate what is known as the "all" flag that lists everything, including all of the folders and files that are hidden from view.

Moving around the terminal

There are some times when you will want to move around the directories using your terminal. Perhaps you want to go from the root section to one of the other directories that you have. To jump to one of the directories that we talked about above, you would just need to type in the command "cd ./Foldername". The cd command is going to let the computer know that you want to move forward relative to your current location.

An alternative that you can use would include specifying the directory with the help of an absolute path. What this means is that the path is going to stay the same regardless of whether you need to go forward or backward to get to the file. To do this, you would just need to type the full directory path, starting from the root and then going all the way to the directory that you would want to be in. An example of this would be "/Users/Name/Documents/".

This step is going to be really useful to you as a beginner. The first thing that you will want to do when you are in a new directory is to take some time to look around. You can type "ls" to list out all the contents that are inside of that new directory. And if you would like to go back to the directory that was above it, you can just type in "cd" to get it done.

Take some time to move to the different directories, using the commands that we have listed out above, so that you can become familiar with it. These commands can be used many times, and they are pretty simple to work with. Just remember that you need to outline exactly what you would like to do to ensure

Chapter 6
Customizing Your Mac with the Terminal

Working with the terminal on your Mac computer will help you to get so much done. It is really simple to use, once you get used to the whole process, and you can gain a lot more power than you would be able to do with your graphical user interface. To see some of the things that you can do with this terminal, we are going to use it to help you customize your Mac computer.

Step 1: Open the terminal

The first thing that you will need to do is open up the terminal. Look at your desktop and search for the spotlight. This should be on the top right hand of the screen at the top of your menu bar. When you click on this, it is going to open up a search bar that shows up in the middle of your screen.

From here, you will need to type in "terminal" and then press on Return. This is going to open up a new terminal window for you to use. If you are not able to find the search icon, you can open up your terminal by using the Finder. To do this, click on Finder, then Applications, Utilities, and then double-click on the Terminal.

Step 2: Use the terminal commands

Now that your terminal window is open, it is time to make some changes. There are a lot of ways that you can customize your Mac computer, as long as you have the right commands to make it work.

The first thing that we are going to do is add a new message to the login screen. All that you will need to do for this one is to type in the following command:

sudo defaults write
/Library/Preferences/com.apple.loginwindow

LoginwindowText "If this laptop is lost, please call 555-555-5555. Cash reward"

When you have this typed in, press the Return button. You can always change out the message that is inside of the quotes to be whatever you would like it to be on your welcome screen. Then the next time that you get to your login screen, you will see this message show up.

You can also decide to add some blank spaces to your doc. To do this is to write out the following command:

defaults write com.apple.dock persistent-apps -array-add '{"tile-type "="spacer-tile";}' killall Dock

Then press Return. This is going to make sure that there is a blank space to your dock each time that this command is entered. You will be able to click and drag the space and move it around in the dock, allowing a divider in for organization. If you are then prompted for your password, you just need to type it in and press Return. If you would like to delete the blank space from your dock, you just need to drag the space out of the dog until it shows "Remove" and then let it go.

There are times when your computer will go to sleep if you are not using it for a certain amount of time. This can be a hassle if you are worried about the computer not staying on long enough to complete the task that you would like. If you want to make sure that the computer will not go to sleep, you just need to type the following command:

Caffeinate

And then press Return. This is going to make sure that the Mac will not fall asleep or log you out just because the computer is not being actively used. If you would then like to allow the Mac to go to sleep again at a later time, like when you are done with the task at hand, you just need to press Control+C, and the terminal will end the caffeinate task.

Next, you can choose to hide a folder. If you made a new folder and called it "HiddenFolder" and you wanted to make sure that no one else can see it, there is a command to help you do this. Let's say that your name is Steve. Use the following command to make it happen:

chflags hidden "/Users/Steve/Desktop/HiddenFolder"

And then press Return. You would, of course, replace the "Steve" with your actual username and then replace "HiddenFolder" with the name of the folder that you would like to hide.

If you would like to make this command a little bit easier, you can also just open up the terminal window and type in "chflags hidden" before dragging and dropping the folder right into the Terminal window before pressing return.

Next, you can change the location of some of your screenshots. The Mac computer is going to save your screenshots on the desktop by default, but you can easily change this if you would like these screenshots to be located in a different folder. We are going to save these on the Desktop in a folder called "Screenshots." Use the following command to make this happen:

defaults write com.apple.screencapture location
"/Users/Steve/Desktop /Screenshots" killall SystemUIServer

And then press Return. You can change the name of the user as well as the name of the folder to work with what you created. For this to work, you must have the folder already created. Otherwise, the screenshots will continue to go to the default of the desktop.

And finally, you can disable your Dashboard completely if you would like. This is something that you would do if you don't use your dashboard at all or if you do not want it to be able to use up the resources on your computer. To disable your dashboard, make sure to use the following command:

defaults write com.apple.dashboard mcx-disabled -boolean yes; killall Dock

And then press Return. If you just want to disable the Dashboard for a little bit, you can always re-enable it at a later time. You will use the exact same command that we have above, but replace the "yes" to "no" and the Dashboard will come back.

These are just a few of the things that you can do with the terminal to personalize the way that your Mac computer works. They may not be the most complicated things that you can do with the command line, but they help to show you what all the terminal can do and can give you some good practice using the terminal. Take some time to practice some of these commands so that you can become more familiar with the terminal and how these commands will work.

Chapter 7
Basic File Management

Now that you have spent some time looking at the MacOS terminal, it is time to learn some of the basic ways to manage files through that terminal. By this, we mean that we are going to learn how to do a few basic file operations such as copying, moving, and opening up the files. If you are interested in giving a few of these a try, it is a good idea to create your own test file. Then if you do something wrong, you will not lose out on important information.

To get started with this, you need to open up TextEdit and then create a new file. We are going to call it "TestFile.txt" to keep things easier, and the folder that you are creating inside of it will be known as "Test". So, let's take a look at some of the different things that you can do when managing your files on the MacOS command line.

Copying

The first thing that we are going to do is learn how to copy a directory or a file. To do this, you will need to use the cp command. This is easier than you would think. Simply open up the command line terminal that you are going to use and then type in the command "cp TestFile.txt TestFile-Copy.txt". This is going to duplicate the file.

What this is going to do is help you to create a new copy of your file inside of the same directory. So, you will end up having two of the same files in the same place if you use the command above. If you want to create a copy of that same file but it needs to be placed in a different directory you would use the command "cp TestFile.txt /Some/Folder/".

Moving

The next thing that you can work on is the moving command. This helps you to take your file and move it over to another directory. This is helpful if you placed the file in the wrong place or you want to share it with others in a new file. The command that you will use for this one is the "mv" command. It will be used the same way that you did with copying. You can also use the mv command to rename your file. The command that you would do to rename your file would be "mv TestFile.txt TestFile-Renamed.txt".

Deleting

You can also use the command line to delete one of the files that you have on your computer. If you accidentally made the file or you are done with it and want to clear up some space on your computer, you would use the delete command to help this happen. The "rm" command will delete your directories and your files. While there are a lot of commands that you can use with this command line, the rm is going to be the most ruthless, and it is really hard to get the file back if you do this command. Make sure that you are using it only on files that you want to permanently get rid of.

Also, if someone has told you to run the command "rm -rf/", do not do this. This is going to delete your files forcefully, and then the file is deleted without asking you for confirmation. We are going to give it a try since we are just working with a test file, but make sure that you really want to get rid of the file ahead of time. To delete a file forcefully, you would type in the command "rm -rf Test".

Chapter 8
What a Profile is and How to Customize It

If you are working on a Mac computer that is all your own, then you do not need to worry about creating a profile as much. But if you share a computer, then it is important to set up profiles for each person who will be on that computer. These profiles can be really nice. They allow you to save your personal information on the computer, and even to personalize or change things on your profile without making these changes to the other profiles. For example, if there is a special program that you only want to have available on your profile, you can do that without affecting the other profiles.

When you share your Mac computer, it is going to be helpful to create a new profile, or account, for each user who is on that computer. Having these separate accounts will allow the individuals to change up the wallpaper and other settings on their account, add in some programs that they use frequently, and to set up the desktop to their own preferences. In addition, you will be able to choose between Standard and Administrator accounts, and there are even some special purpose accounts, like Managed Accounts that will make it easier for you to add in Parental Controls and other special features.

If you need to set up these accounts, you will find that the steps to get it done can be pretty simple. Some of the steps that you need to take include:

- Turn on the computer and get it all set up. When the computer is on, click on the Apple menu and then choose System Preferences. If this does not work, you can also click on your Applications folder on your Dock and then scroll down to System Preferences before selecting the icon.

- From here, you can click on the Users and Groups or the Accounts. Look for which one is present because it will depend on the OS version you are using. Once you click on that, you can click on the Lock icon, located in the lower left of your Accounts window. Then enter your password before clicking OK.

- Now you will need to click the "+" sign under your Account list. This is going to allow you to set up a new account. You can pick which kind of account you would like to select from the "New Account" drop-down menu.

- At this point, you will need to type in the name of the new user under the "Full Name' text box. You can also type in the account name, which is going to be the new login name for the user. Type this login name into the Account Name text box.

- Here you will need to type in a new password to help keep the new profile safe and secure. You can choose which password you would like to use, or you can click on the Password Assistant. This icon is going to help you out because it will create a random password of the type and length that you ask for. You can type in the password to the Verify box. Make sure that you enter a good hint into the Password Hint box before clicking to Create Account.

- If you are someone who gets onto your profile without using a password, then take a moment to click "Turn Off Automatic Login"> If you forget to do this, the computer is automatically going to open up your account, regardless of who is on the computer. That user would be able to get ahold of all your information as they would need to log out of your profile before they could log in to theirs. Make sure to click the Lock icon.

- Take some time to check whether the new account is working the proper way. You can click on your Apple icon and log out of the account. From here, you will log in with the new username and password that you created. When you can confirm that this new account is working properly, you can begin to work on it, give it to the person who will use that account, or log out and go back to your original account.

And that is all that you need to know to get started with creating new profiles on your Mac computer. This can be helpful if you plan to have more than one user on the same computer and you want to make sure that you keep your information separate from each other. It really only takes a few minutes to get the new profile set up and tested, and you can create as many of these profiles as you would like.

Personalizing your profile

Now that you have your own profile on the Mac computer, it is time to start adding some personalization. You can have a little fun with this and change up as many things as you would like inside of it. This can also be a good way to distinguish your account from one of the other accounts to make it easier to know whether you are in the right place or not. Some of the ways that you can personalize your profile includes:

New wallpaper

You can choose which wallpaper you would like to use. This can be something that is nice and simple to look at, or you can pick out a picture that you would like to add in there. To set up the right wallpaper, you will just need to visit General, then Desktop and Screen Saver, and then Desktop before picking out the option that you would like to have on your computer.

Custom color scheme

When you are picking out a color scheme, you will find that the Apple program is only going to provide you with one other color besides the default one. It is known as Graphite, and you can find it under System Preferences, General, and Appearance. The best way for you to get a different color scheme is to activate an app-specific theme. For example, if you are using Alfred to help control your Mac and you have already activated Powerpack, you can use a custom theme to change the way that Alfred looks.

If you would like to add a sleeker look to the menu bar, you will be able to set it so that it appears black. You can do this by clicking on System Preferences and then General before selecting on Use dark menu bar and Dock to make it happen. You can also pick out the color for your highlighted text by selecting (from the same menu) Highlight color and picking from the drop-down menu.

Changing the icons

You can scale your icons up and down and even change the way that they look, and you can do all of this without needing to bring in a third party to help get it done. If you would like to scale your icons up or down, you will need to click on View, Show View Options, and Icon Size.

To use one of your custom images as a folder icon, which can make the folders easier to see and recognize, then you will first need to copy that image over to the clipboard. Then you can go into Finder to select the folder that will get the new icon. Once you have found the folder, click on File and then Get Info.

In the box that opens up, you can click on the icon at the top and then click Edit and Paste. At this point, the custom icon should be in place. If you do not like how the icon looks or you picked out the wrong picture, you can select it and then hit the delete key so that you go back to the default icon.

Better login screen

It is even possible to add some personalization to your login screen when you are using a Mac. You will need to replace your default image and the user picture for your account. It is even possible to add a new message to the lock screen.

If you would like to switch out the login background, you first need to find the picture that you would like to use. It needs to be a .PNG image that also matches the resolution of the Mac display. You can take an existing image and then crop it to fit into the right place, or you can download the image that you like from the web. If you are getting an image from the Web, make sure that there are no copyright restrictions on it. We are going to name that image com.apple.desktop.admin.png.

If you are looking for a picture and you are not sure what the display resolution of your Mac is, you can easily find this. Just open the command line and then look under Apple, About This Mac, and then Displays.

Now you need to navigate to the Caches folder. This is found in the main library of the Mac, so the /Library/Caches. From here you will be able to find the picture file that we saved earlier. Make sure that you back it up somewhere safe and then replace it with the custom image file. If it all goes well, the next time that you restart the Mac, the image that you picked out is going to be in the background for your login screen.

You can also do this with your user picture. To replace the default picture, you will need to click on System Preferences, Users and Groups, and Password. You can click the picture that is already there and then swap it out for any other picture that you would like to use. Make sure to hit Save to make sure that the selected picture is saved on your screen the proper way.

Now, if you would like to set a new message for your lock screen, you just need to add a few steps as well. To do this, visit System Preferences, Security and Privacy, and General. You can then select the first box next to Show a message when the screen is locked. If this option is already grayed out, you will need to click on your lock icon (found at the bottom of the pain), so that you can enter the system password and give yourself access to this setting.

Next, you can click on the Set Lock Message and then type in the message that you want your lock screen to say. Hit OK. You will need to restart the Mac, but the next time that you do, this message is going to show up at the bottom of the screen. You will see it right above the power options.

Custom sounds

And finally, we are going to take a look at how you can customize some of the sounds that you can hear on your profile. You are not limited to only changing visualize things when you want to personalize. You can easily add some different audio tweaks as well. To start, we are going to change the system voice from the default. To do this, you can click on System Preferences, Accessibility, Speech, System Voice. From here, you will be able to choose a new sound for your alerts by clicking on System Preferences, Sound, Sound Effects.

There are a lot of different things that you can do here. For example, you can even set the Mac so that it announced the time in a voice of your choice each hour. To do this, you would just need to select System Preferences, Date and Time, and Clock. Set it up so that the right voice will alert you of the time at each hour (or every few hours if that works best for your schedule). This is just one of the ways that you can change up some of the audio that you can hear on your computer.

As you can see, there are a lot of different ways that you can personalize your profile and make it look and act the way that you want. And if you are one of many profiles, you will be able to make these changes without having to worry about it making the same changes on another profile. Make sure to try out a few of these personalization's to make your computer as unique as you are.

Chapter 9
How to Troubleshoot Your Mac with the Command Line

There are times when your computer is not going to act the way that you would like. Perhaps some of the programs are not running how you want, or it is going slow, or something else is wrong. Knowing how to troubleshoot your own computer can help to make it last longer and can even save you some money compared to going to a professional. The good news is that using the command line will make it easier for you to troubleshoot your Mac computer, even if you do not have a ton of experience doing this on your own. Let's take a look at some of the ways that you can troubleshoot your Mac computer all on your own.

Ipconfig

The first thing that we need to do is open up the terminal and then take a look at all the interface information that is present on the computer. You can type in ipconfig to see this information. Some of the information that will come up includes the DNS servers and routers, the subnet masks, the LAN IP, and more. You can also use this command to configure the network settings.

If you are the administrator of the computer and you have worked with the Windows ipconfig in the past, the OS X ipconfig is going to be pretty much the same thing. This command is not one that you should use for any other reason besides testing and debugging the system, otherwise, it will start to cause some problems.

If you would like to display the IP address for the wireless network (which will be denoted by en1), you need to enter the following command:

Ipconfig getifaddr en0

If you would like to display the interface's subnet mask, you will need to enter the following command:

Ipconfig getoption en1 sunet_mask

If you would like to take a look at the DNS and determine if the interface has been set to leverage, you would need to enter the following command:

Ipconfig gtoption en1 domain_name_server

To figure out the router and the DHCP information that is supplied to the Mac computer, you would need to enter the following command:

Ipconfig getpacket en1

Traceroute

Another thing that you can do is the traceroute command. One of the most trying of the network failures to diagnose as well as to repair is a failure to connect to a network outside the organization. To run the traceroute command from the location of our Mac over to the destination resource, you will need to use the following command (making sure to substitute your intended address in place of the google.com):

Traceroute google.com

When you use this one, the command is going to print out all of the results of each step from your computer to the destination address. It will also note the IP addresses that this path crosses along the way and the latency delays that are encountered at each stop. With all of this information at hand, you will be able to see right away where the issue is occurring and you can figure out how to make it better.

These are just two of the ways that you can troubleshoot some of the issues that may come up on your computer. The first one is going to allow you a chance to look at what is going on with your computer so you can see where some of the issues may be coming from. There is a lot of information present here, and that can make it easier for you to know where to start with the troubleshooting.

The second command is going to be useful if you are trying to get onto a website or another place that is outside your network, and you want to know what it is running into issues. The traceroute command will provide you with all of the steps that your computer has to take to get to the other location, and this command will list out all of the places where an issue can occur. You may find that the issue is somewhere with your system, somewhere with the host you are trying to reach, or located in another place.

Of course, before you get started with any kind of troubleshooting, you need to make sure that you do some basic steps first. If the computer is acting funny, running slowly, or something else seems like it is off, you should first try restarting the computer. This often takes care of a lot of the issues that your computer is having. If you do that and it doesn't work, then move on to some of the troubleshooting that we talked about before.

Many people are not sure how to fix their computers if something goes wrong. The hope that they can get it to work or that they can find a professional to do the work for them. But when you start learning how to use the command line, you can do some of the troubleshooting on your own.

Conclusion

Thanks again for taking the time to download this book!

You should now have a good understanding of the command line for the Mac operating system and how to make it work for your needs. You may be used to working with the graphical user interface, the one where you simply click on an icon to tell the computer how to behave, but you will quickly find that working with the command line can make life so much easier.

This guidebook provided you with all the information that you needed to start using the command line on your Mac computer. We discussed what the command line was, how to open up the terminal to get started, and some of the commands that you can use inside your terminal to open and close files, to troubleshoot issues on your computer, and even to personalize your computer the way that you would like it to be.

When you are ready to start learning more about the command line and how it can work for your needs, make sure to check out this guidebook to help you get started.

If you enjoyed this book, please take the time to leave me a review on Amazon. I appreciate your honest feedback, and it really helps me to continue producing high-quality books.

www.ingramcontent.com/pod-product-compliance
Lightning Source LLC
LaVergne TN
LVHW052126070326
832902LV00038B/3957